OXFORD

Revising AQA GCSE
English

Rachel Redford

Specification **B**

AQA GCSE English

Foundation and Higher Tiers

OXFORD
UNIVERSITY PRESS

Great Clarendon Street, Oxford OX2 6DP

Oxford University Press is a department of the University of Oxford.
It furthers the University's objective of excellence in research, scholarship,
and education by publishing worldwide in

Oxford New York

Auckland Bangkok Buenos Aires Cape Town Chennai
Dar es Salaam Delhi Hong Kong Istanbul Karachi Kolkata
Kuala Lumpur Madrid Melbourne Mexico City Mumbai Nairobi
São Paulo Shanghai Taipei Tokyo Toronto

Oxford is a registered trade mark of Oxford University Press
in the UK and in certain other countries

British Library Cataloguing in Publication Data

Data available

ISBN 0 19 832059 0

1 3 5 7 9 10 8 6 4 2

Printed in Italy by Rotolito Lombarda

Acknowledgements

We are grateful for permission to include the following copyright material:

Assumpta Acam-Otura: '[Arise to] The Day's Toil' from *The Heinemann Book of African Women's Poetry* edited by Stella and Frank Chipasula (Heinemann Educational 1995), reprinted by permission of Heinemann, part of Harcourt Education Ltd.

Moniza Alvi: 'Exile' from *Carrying My Wife* (Bloodaxe Books, 2000), reprinted by permission of the publishers.

Dea Birkett: extract from 'Are you a tourist or a traveller?', *The Guardian*, Travel, 24.08.02, copyright © Dea Birkett 2002, reprinted by permission of Guardian Newspapers Ltd.

Anthony Bourdain: extract from *Kitchen Confidential* (Bloomsbury, 2000), reprinted by permission of the publisher.

Mark Brown: 'Wild wild west' from *The Guardian*, Travel, 21.10.00, copyright © The Guardian 2000, reprinted by permission of Guardian Newspapers Ltd.

Joe Eszterhas: extracts from 'Hollywood's Responsibility for Smoking Deaths' first published in *New York Times*, 9.8.02, reprinted by permission of *The New York Times*.

David Harrison: 'Sherpas risk death for British trekkers' from *The Sunday Telegraph* 30.6.02, © Telegraph Group Ltd 2002, reprinted by permission of the Telegraph Group Ltd.

Shakuntala Hawoldar: 'To My Little Girl' from *The Heinemann Book of African Women's Poetry* edited by Stella and Frank Chipasula (Heinemann Educational 1995), reprinted by permission of Heinemann, part of Harcourt Education Ltd.

Charlotte Hobson: extract from *Black Earth City: A Year in the Heart of Russia* (Granta Books, 2001), reprinted by permission of the publisher.

Felicity Kendal: extract from *White Cargo* (Michael Joseph, 1998), copyright © Felicity Kendal 1998, reprinted by permission of Penguin Books Ltd.

Ian McDonald: lines from 'Yusuman Ali, Charcoal Seller' from *Jaffo, The Calypsonian* (Peepal Tree Books, 1994), reprinted by permission of the publisher.

Andrew Marr: extract from *Viewpoint* article 'You've never had it so good' from *The Big Issue*, August 5-11, 2002, reprinted by permission of The Big Issue Company Ltd.

Nicholas Pyke: extract from 'Girls in trousers: an issue for EOC' from *The Guardian*, 4.7.02, copyright © Nicholas Pyke 2002, reprinted by permission of Guardian Newspapers Ltd.

Tim Severin: extract from *Seeking Robinson Crusoe* (Macmillan, 2002), reprinted by permission of Pan Macmillan Ltd, London.

Nick Squires: 'Wildlife pays price after drought sweeps Australia' from *The Sunday Telegraph* 21.7.02, © Telegraph Group Ltd 2002, reprinted by permission of the Telegraph Group Ltd.

John Watts: extracts from 'Japan takes bear of little brain to its heart' from *The Guardian*, Finance, 30.8.02, copyright © John Watts 2002, reprinted by permission of Guardian Newspapers Ltd.

Although we have tried to trace and contact all copyright holders, this has not always been possible. If notified, the publisher undertakes to rectify any errors or omissions at the earliest opportunity.

The publisher would like to thank the following for permission to reproduce photographs: Corbis/Richard List (page 32); Newspix Australia (page 36).

CONTENTS

This *Revision Guide* is for both Foundation Tier and Higher Tier GCSE English students. It contains separate guidance, tasks, and skills practice for each tier. Each unit presents short, entertaining, and extremely attractive texts to encourage reluctant or slow readers on the Foundation Tier, and to challenge Higher Tier students. The detailed guidance, advice, and examples are carefully structured to **improve students' skills** and **raise their GCSE grades**.

It is designed to be valuable for *all* students. It is, of course, for students at school, but it also offers essential guidance to adult learners, return-to-study and re-take students; distance learners; students in special units or isolated centres; and home-educated students. Studied alongside its companion *English Students' Book,* it represents a comprehensive preparation for GCSE English examinations for all students.

Students of all abilities will benefit, as it provides teaching on basic skills as well as guidance on sophisticated and challenging tasks. All the examination assessment objectives have been incorporated into the guidance and the tasks, without burdening the students with jargon.

The *Revision Guide* provides opportunities for students to:

◆ understand and practise exactly what is required of them in the English examinations
◆ work at their own pace and in their own time
◆ practise and improve their basic skills
◆ benefit from a wide range of guidance, practical advice, and examples
◆ gain from studying examples of students' work
◆ practise their reading-with-understanding skills
◆ try reading texts with understanding within a time limit
◆ read a wide variety of appealing and accessible prose and poetry texts
◆ write both brief and extended responses to tasks
◆ practise detailed writing skills required in the examination
◆ work through a complete set of sample examination papers.

SECTION 1 REVISING SKILLS

Errors with basic skills cost candidates precious marks, and frequently prevent them from achieving a grade C. This section gives full explanations and examples of a range of these basic skills. They are interspersed with lively exercises and tasks for students to work through at their own pace and to self-correct.

The basic skills in this section include: pronouns, question marks, exclamation marks, apostrophes, spelling, and commonly confused words.

SECTION 2 EXAM PRACTICE

Reading

In accordance with the requirements of the examination, each tier has three separate reading units on media, non-fiction, and poetry from different cultures. The varied texts provided in each unit have been chosen to appeal to even the most jaded student! The guidance is structured to enable students to **analyse and interpret content and language**, and to **write focused and relevant answers in the examination**.

The skills include:

Higher Tier: making contrasts and comparisons; interpreting media content and sources; interpreting metaphor

Foundation Tier: responding to key words in the question; analysing media headlines; making analytical language points.

Writing

In accordance with the requirements of the examination, each tier concentrates on the two writing 'triplets': **argue, persuade, advise** and **analyse, review, comment**. Punchy, engaging texts are used to illustrate writing features and skills, and students are set writing tasks arising from what they have just learned.

The skills include:

Higher Tier: arguing with flair; engaging the audience; analysing and commenting on opinions

Foundation Tier: organizing a persuasive argument; making comments and analysing opinions; writing in continuous prose.

SECTION 3 SAMPLE PAPERS

A complete set of papers and pre-released texts for each tier is provided, and students can work through them in their own time. This gives invaluable practice in **timing** as well as making students familiar with the layout and the requirements of the examination papers. It is a great advantage to candidates if they know before they enter the examination room how many minutes they have for writing their answers to each question – and have had practice in timing themselves. It is extremely important to build into the timing of their questions about five minutes to think about and organize the topic at the beginning, and, in the Writing questions, an extra five minutes to check for errors at the end.

The sample papers comprise:

◆ **Pre-released texts:** media texts and poetry from different cultures. Students can spend as long as they like on these and discuss them with anyone willing to join in.
◆ **Paper 1 for Foundation Tier and Higher Tier** with different unseen texts for each tier. This should be timed at 1 hour 40 minutes.
◆ **Paper 2 for Foundation Tier and Higher Tier** with different unseen texts for each tier. This should be timed at 1 hour 30 minutes.

DON'T CONFUSE YOUR PRONOUNS

Personal subjective	Objective	Possessive	Reflexive
Singular (one person or thing)			
I	me	mine	myself
you	you	yours	yourself
he	him	his	himself
she	her	hers	herself
it	it	its	itself
Plural (more than one person or thing)			
we	us	ours	ourselves
you	you	yours	yourselves
they	them	theirs	themselves

Explanation

Personal subjective pronouns are used for the subject of a sentence – when someone (or something) does the 'action' of the verb:
She is a brilliant surgeon.
He stood behind the shed door.

Objective pronouns are used when someone (or something) has the 'action' of the verb done to them:
Chris told her about the situation.
Minty saw him behind the shed door.

Possessive pronouns are used when something belongs to someone (or something):
Those footmarks are yours, not mine.

Reflexive pronouns are used:
a) when someone (or something) does something to or by themselves:
The exotic bird spent hours grooming itself.

b) for emphasis:
They didn't seem to care but I, myself, was embarrassed.

- ◆ Check the spelling of all these words.
- ◆ Notice that **none** of them has an apostrophe!

The word **it's** does not belong in this list. The apostrophe shows that a letter has been left out. **It's** means **it is** or **it has**:
It's a great opportunity for me.
It's been raining.

Now write your own sentences using all the pronouns in the above grid.

- ◆ Underline or highlight all the pronouns.
- ◆ Remember your full stops at the end of each sentence!

The first few have been done for you.

1 I was devastated when you said goodbye to **me**. I thought you were **mine** forever, but I was deceiving **myself**.
2 **You** told me to meet **you** at six o'clock, not eight. The mistake is **yours** and you have only **yourself** to blame.
3 **He** was . . .

QUESTIONS AND EXCLAMATION MARKS – GET THEM RIGHT

A sentence with an **exclamation mark** at the end jumps out from the page. This punctuation mark has many uses. It can, for example, emphasize strong emotions such as amazement:
Wow! I just can't believe it!

It can signal a command:
Come here this minute!

It can give emphasis:
No!

It can indicate that something is ridiculous or funny:
And then he ate it!

◆ Use *one* exclamation mark, not two or three in a row.
◆ Don't over-use exclamation marks – use them sparingly and they will be more effective.
◆ Don't include a full stop as well as an exclamation mark.

A **question mark** shows that your sentence is asking a question. When the sentence is short, it's easy to remember the question mark:
How many GCSEs did you pass?

When you are writing a long sentence, you might forget the question mark at the end. Always check that you have included it:
How would you like to be imprisoned in a cage, lose your freedom to run or lie in the sun, and have noisy people staring and pointing at you all day long?

◆ Don't forget to include question marks.
◆ A question mark, like an exclamation mark, replaces a full stop, so don't use a full stop as well.

Now read this account of a true incident:

Yesterday, a 17-year-old girl tried to smuggle her pet chameleon into Britain from Dubai – by wearing the creature as a hat. While her fellow passengers were waiting for their luggage at the carousel at Manchester Airport, those standing close to her noticed that the girl's hat was not merely strange – it was *alive!*

'At first, I thought it was plastic,' said passenger David Westbury. 'But then its tongue flicked out! You just wouldn't believe it, would you?'

'How can you wear a chameleon on your head all the way from Dubai without the air crew noticing?' asked Martha Gallop, another passenger. 'It's amazing!'

A Customs spokesman said: 'Chameleons are an endangered species. It's an offence to bring in animals from abroad. This one will be looked after until a decision is made about its future.'

◆ Highlight all the pronouns in the text.
◆ In a different colour, highlight **it's**. You will find it used twice. What is the difference in meaning between **it's** and **its**?
◆ Write three sentences including **it's** and three sentences including **its**.

Now, use what you have learned about pronouns, exclamation marks, and question marks to complete the following task.

The Customs Officer is interviewing the 17-year-old girl who tried to smuggle her chameleon into Britain.

Make a list of ten questions he might ask her along with her ten replies to the questions.

In your sentences:
◆ use exclamation marks
◆ use question marks
◆ highlight or underline the pronouns
◆ put quotation marks around what the Officer says and what the girl says
◆ put full stops in the right places.

The task has been started for you:

The Customs Officer's Questions

1 'Is this creature **yours**?'
2 'Did **you** bring **it** for **yourself**, or was **it** for someone else?"
3 'What . . .

The girl's replies

'Yes, **I'm** afraid **it** is.'
'**It's** mine! **It's** my pet.'

DON'T MAKE MISTAKES WITH APOSTROPHES

Read the following factual report.

Killer bears on the loose

Ola is a rundown town on Russia's far-east coast. This summer its inhabitants have been living in fear. The town is right in the path of the wild bears' hunt for fish. This year, forest fires have destroyed the bears' feeding grounds to the west, and humpback salmon, which is the animals' staple diet, have been in short supply. This means that the bears have been forced into the humans' territory to hunt for food.

Two brothers, Alexander and Nikolai, were poaching on the river bank. They heard a sound which they thought was the fishing inspector's footsteps. They looked up to see a massive bear standing seven feet high on its hind legs. After a moment of paralysis when they couldn't move for terror, they fled for their lives. Alexander managed to scramble up a tree from where he could hear Nikolai's screams as he carried on running. But a bear will always out-run a man. Nikolai didn't make it home.

A police helicopter has since logged seventeen bears roaming the town's outskirts. 'It's a tragedy for the town,' a police officer said. 'We're surrounded by hungry bears. It's difficult to reassure the public.'

Traps have been set for the bears but they haven't been very successful. Only four bears have been caught and killed.

The people of Ola now fear to go outdoors.

Apostrophes are used for two reasons:

1 Omission – to show where a letter or letters have been left out:
we're (the letter 'a' has been left out of *we are*)

2 Possession – to show that something belongs to someone or something:
Nikolai's screams (the screams belong to Nikolai)

Apostrophes are **not** used in plural nouns where there is no possession.
Study the following explanation of singular and plural nouns:

> *Bear* = singular noun, just one. *Bears* = plural noun, more than one.
> To make a noun plural, we usually add an 's', but not always:
> *Man* = singular noun. *Men* = plural noun.
> Make sure you know what a singular noun is and what a plural noun is.

Write out the following two sentences, and underline the seven plural nouns:

There were groups of wild, hungry bears roaming around the villages.
The two brothers were victims of several attacks from the wild animals.

You should have underlined
groups/bears/villages/brothers/victims/attacks/animals

Why are there no apostrophes in these words? Because they are **plural nouns** and nothing **belongs to them**.

Make two columns headed *Omission* and *Possession* and list all the words from the text 'Killer bears on the loose' which have apostrophes, putting them in the appropriate columns. Start this way:

Omission	Possession
Couldn't	Russia's

Note that in **possession**, the apostrophe 's' goes after the singular form of the noun if something belongs to one person or thing:

The poacher's hideaway was discovered (belongs to one poacher)
James's shirt was ruined (belongs to James)

The apostrophe 's' goes after the plural form of the noun if something belongs to more than one person or thing:

The poachers' hideaway was discovered (belongs to more than one poacher)

Candidates often make mistakes with the apostrophes for **omission** in verbs.

Complete form	Contracted or short form
it is	it's: *It's a great day for fishing*
it has	it's: *It's been a great success*
we are	we're: *We're winning!*
you are	you're: *You're a star!*
we had	we'd: *We'd been there a year*

Take care with **negative verbs** (the 'not' form).

cannot	can't: *I can't understand you*
will not	won't: *He won't do as I say*
are not	aren't: *Aren't they coming with us?*
could not	couldn't: *She couldn't bear to look*
do not	don't: *Don't kick it, it might explode!*
does not	doesn't: *It doesn't work any more*

Note this one:

would have/could have   would've/could've
*I **would have** stayed longer if Karen had been there.*
*I **would've** stayed longer.*
*You **could have** done really well if you had tried.*
*You **could've** done really well.*

There is no such form as 'could of' or 'would of' — these are *wrong*.

◆ In the columns you have made for Omission and Possession, add five more examples of your own of words with apostrophes.
◆ Write some sentences using all the contracted verb forms in the list above. Highlight the contracted verb forms in your sentences and check that the apostrophes are in the right places.
◆ In the examination, remember: if you're not sure about an apostrophe, it is better to leave it out altogether than put it in the wrong place!

Writing tag questions

A tag is the little tail which, when put on the end of a statement, turns it into a question. We ask tag questions when we speak, and we write them in direct speech:

Statement: *The bear was gigantic.*
Statement with tag question: *The bear was gigantic, wasn't it?*

Wasn't it? is the tag which makes the statement into a question.

Here are some examples of tag questions:

The trappers have killed only four bears so far, haven't they?
It's not safe to go out now, is it?

Now write five tag questions of your own. Remember to:

◆ put the apostrophe in the right place
◆ include a comma before your tag
◆ put a question mark at the end of your question.

Look who's talking!

Don't confuse these two words which sound the same: **who's** and **whose**.

Who's means **who is** or **who has**:
Who's that hiding up the tree?
The young man who's been hiding up the tree is terrified.

If you can replace *who's* with *who is* or *who has* without changing the sense of the sentence, then you know you need that apostrophe for omission.

Whose is a relative pronoun like **who** and **which**.

Which introduces a clause telling you more about some*thing* in the sentence. **Who** and **whose** introduce a clause telling you more about a *person* in the sentence.

*Alexander, <u>**whose** brother was a victim of the hungry bear</u>, was devastated.*
*Alexander, <u>**who** lost his brother last year in an accident</u>, is not the boy he used to be.*

The underlined clauses introduced by **whose** and **who** tell you more about the person, Alexander.

*The tree, <u>**which** Alexander climbed to escape the bear</u>, saved his life.*

The underlined clause introduced by **which** tells you more about the thing, the tree.

On its own, **whose** means 'to whom':

Whose are these shoes? (To whom do these shoes belong?)

You can *never* replace **whose** with **who is** or **who has**.

Copy these sentences and fill the gaps with either **who's** or **whose**:

'. . . been sleeping in *my* bed? And . . . are these great big footprints? It's a BEAR . . . been here! I swear it's that big black bear . . . face was peering in the window yesterday,' cried Goldilocks in astonishment.

Now write five sentences of your own using **who's**, and five sentences using **whose**.

DON'T MAKE BASIC SPELLING MISTAKES

Spelling words like *translucent*, *synthetic*, *psyche*, *suicidal,* or *serenity* wrongly is not a great crime – an examiner would be pleased to see you using such words.

Spelling words in common use wrongly, however, will definitely lose you marks. English spelling has rules, but often words don't follow the spelling rules and you just have to **learn** the spellings.

The more you read, the more you will know when a word 'looks wrong'.

Words that sound similar often confuse candidates:

feel – fill – full – fulfil
*I don't **feel** well – **Fill** the tank **full**, please – Please help me **fulfil** my dream*
Write your own examples using these words.

being – been
*She was **being** very unkind – We're all human **beings**, after all – Have you **been** on that new ride yet?*
Write your own examples using these words.

choose – choice – chose
***Choose** whichever filling you want – It's your **choice** – Yesterday they **chose** to enter the race.*
Write your own examples using these words.

lose – losing – loose
*You'll **lose** your way in the forest – The horse was **losing** the race when it fell – The bears are **loose** and dangerous.*
Write your own examples using these words.

our – are
***Our** memories of Jack **are** happy ones.*
Write your own examples using these words.

quite – quiet
*His voice was **quite** good, but not good enough to go forward to the final – Be **quiet**, I'm trying to think!*
Write your own examples using these words.

Don't **ever** spell these words wrongly:

◆ **their** (belonging to them: *Their legs are very long*)
How to remember it: *Them* and *their* both begin with *the*

◆ **there** (the place: *over there*)
How to remember it: Think of **here**, **there** and *everywhere* – they are all places and all have *here* in them

◆ **does** and **doesn't**

◆ **writing** – don't be tempted to double the 't' or include an 'e'

◆ **know** – know when to write 'no'!

Some useful spelling patterns
◆ Words ending in –*ment*, such as *amusement*
the ending –*ment* is added to a verb to make a noun:
govern + *ment* = *government* (note the 'n' and 'm')
excite + *ment* = *excitement* (note the 'e' is kept)
encourage + *ment* = *encouragement*
state + *ment* = *statement*
Add your own examples. Remember this exception:
Argue + *ment* = *argument* (the 'e' is dropped)

◆ Words ending in –*ly*
the ending –*ly* is added to an adjective to make an adverb, such as *quickly*
unfortunate + *ly* = *unfortunately* (note the 'e' + ly)
quiet + *ly* = *quietly*

similar + *ly* = *similarly*
usual + *ly* = *usually* (note the double 'l')
hopeful + *ly* = *hopefully*
real + *ly* = *really*
Add your own examples.

◆ Verbs ending in *–ing*
To make the *–ing* form of a verb (such as *swiping*) from a verb which ends in silent 'e'(such as *to swipe*), drop the 'e' and add *–ing*. **Note**: a final silent 'e' is an 'e' which is not pronounced)
like + *ing* = *liking*
have + *ing* = *having*
come + *ing* = *coming*
smile + *ing* = *smiling*
Add your own examples.

Top 25 spellings to learn				
1) desperate	6) pursue	11) privilege	16) independence	21) unconscious
2) disappointed	7) believe	12) controversial	17) embarrassing	22) discipline
3) decision	8) business	13) confront	18) threatened	23) repetition
4) safety	9) benefit	14) disappearance	19) poison	24) conscience
5) boredom	10) opportunity	15) experience	20) resolve	25) competition

Learn five a day! Write a sentence for each of these 25 words.

Revise this section on apostrophes and spellings, and as well as the 25 words above, include in your 25 sentences:

◆ you're/your
◆ does/doesn't
◆ could have
◆ would've
◆ their/there
◆ who's/whose
◆ choose/loose/lose/chose
◆ fulfil
◆ nouns ending in *–ment*
◆ adverbs ending in *–ly*
◆ verbs ending in *–ing*

Underline all these key words and check their spellings carefully. If they need apostrophes, make sure you put them in the right places.

EXAM PRACTICE

READING RESPONSE TO PRE-RELEASE MEDIA

Interpreting content and sources

Read this extract from a newspaper article:

Japan takes bear of little brain to its heart

Jonathan Watts in Tokyo

Winnie the Pooh might seem a rather unlikely modern hero for Japan, but according to the latest monthly 'hit chart' – a Top of the Pops of cute cartoon animals – Pooh-san became Japan's best-selling character this summer.

'Pooh seems to fit Japan right now – he makes people feel at ease in troubled times,' said Kazuo Rikukawa, director of Character Databank which produces the chart. 'He is comfortably imperfect, whereas Mickey Mouse is exhaustingly energetic and strong-willed.'

At Tokyo's Disney resort – the world's most popular theme park – Mickey always used to reign supreme, but now the crowds flock first to Winnie the Pooh. Despite a queuing time of more than two hours, the park's most popular attraction is 'Hunny Hunt', a ride through the 100 Acre Wood which opened two years ago.

To meet the extra demand generated by this ride and the Tigger Movie, Disney company stores in Japan have established Just Pooh corners. They are almost as popular among young women as small children.

'Mickey is still our main character, but in terms of sales, Pooh has taken over,' said Rieko Tsukakoshi of the company's head office. 'Everyone wants to cuddle him. He has a kind of soothing quality that people like.'

Although there has been a mini-boom for all things English since David Beckham charmed Japan during the World Cup, the successful marketing of Winnie the Pooh is not so much linked to Anglophilia as it is to the bear's easy-going nature and fashionable allergy to hard work.

According to consumer analysts, this flawed, but laid-back, personality appeals to teens and 20-somethings who are reluctant to follow the workaholic lifestyles of their parents.

1 Why is Pooh Bear popular with adults and young people in Japan?

Candidates often waste a great deal of time in the examination on straightforward questions like these because they fail to **select** the appropriate points, and include **narrative** and **irrelevant** material. Read the question carefully and identify **key words** – here the key words are *Why* and *with adults and young people*.

Examiners want to see that you have understood the text. They don't want you to re-tell the story or describe the information, but to **interpret** it so you can answer the **why** part of the question.

Quoting the words of the director of the Character Databank, a candidate writes:

> Pooh Bear is popular with adults and young people in Japan because he is a flawed character. Japan is going through difficult times and people feel comforted by cuddly Pooh Bear. The Japanese love him because he is 'comfortably imperfect', whereas Mickey Mouse with his relentless energy no longer appeals.

Examiner's checklist on the candidate's response:

- ✔ understands why Pooh appeals
- ✔ expresses reasons clearly
- ✔ interprets text without merely copying words and phrases
- ✔ quotes briefly and aptly from the text
- ✔ selects appropriate detail from the text
- ✔ uses the example of Mickey Mouse to strengthen the point
- ✔ expression is economical
- ✔ there is no irrelevance or unfocused description.

Now answer Question 1 on your own, using the above example to guide you.

2   How does Jonathan Watts' choice of sources affect the reader?

What are writers' **sources**? Quite simply, sources are where they get the information from to write the article, and to support their views and ideas.

Writers might:

- ◆ interview someone in authority, or an eye witness
- ◆ do research on the Internet
- ◆ quote facts and figures issued by a company
- ◆ include a graph
- ◆ quote statistics issued by a government department
- ◆ select facts from a report or newspaper article
- ◆ draw on personal experience and letters, or entries in a diary.

All these examples are possible sources for writers.

First, identify the writer's sources in this text:

- ◆ the director of Character Databank
- ◆ Rieko Tsukakoshi from the Disney company's head office
- ◆ consumer analysts.

Consider the following reasons why writers might use particular sources in their writing:

- ◆ to reassure/impress their readers
- ◆ to add apparent or genuine validity to the writing
- ◆ to extend the argument/facts/information/thesis of the writing
- ◆ deliberately to confuse/misinform readers or to reinforce prejudices
- ◆ to elucidate and clarify complex ideas or information.

Perhaps you can think of examples and add more reasons.

Now, refer back to the text and use the prompts above to help you answer Question 2.

Direct speech and headlines

Read this newspaper report.

Doggy paddles home

Paddy, the black Labrador, loves nothing better than going out on the motor cruiser with his master, Stephen le Crocq.

'He's just wild about sea water! He'll always stand at the front of the deck where he'll catch the spray,' Stephen explained as he hugged his wonder-dog yesterday.

Stephen was cruising with Paddy at the weekend a mile off the Isle of Wight when the dog disappeared. Stephen realized he must have slipped off the wet deck. When he failed to find Paddy, he put out a call to other boat crews to keep an eye out for the two-year old Labrador.

'I blamed myself,' explained Stephen. 'Usually Paddy wears his specially made orange life-jacket but, because it was hot, I didn't make him wear it.'

After five hours of unsuccessful searching, Stephen docked at Cowes in the Isle of Wight.

'I knew I'd lost Paddy and it was my fault. I was gutted,' he said.

But, unknown to Stephen, ten miles away across one of the world's busiest waterways, Paddy was lying exhausted on the beach not far from his home in the New Forest. He was found and taken to a vet who identified Paddy through his microchip, and Stephen and Paddy were reunited.

'I couldn't believe it when I got the call!' Stephen said, smiling. 'Strong currents, ferries, tankers, liners – he'd dodged the lot and swum for six hours to get home. What a star!'

The vet who examined Paddy said: 'He's a very fit and strong dog. Even so, it is absolutely amazing that he should have swum so far to safety across that dangerous stretch of water.'

1 What is the effect of the direct speech in this newspaper report?

First of all, remind yourself of the difference between direct speech and reported speech. Direct speech uses speech marks around what someone actually says: *'I blamed myself,' explained Stephen.*

Reported speech has no speech marks, but **reports** what is being said: *Stephen explained that he blamed himself.*

◆ Write down three more examples of direct speech from the text.
◆ Re-write your examples as reported speech.
◆ What differences do you see in the **effect** of the two kinds of speech? To answer this question, you could say:

Direct speech is more dramatic than reported speech. 'What a star!' is a dramatic piece of direct speech because it's an exclamation. It is dramatic because it is colloquial, and therefore more informal and lively than reported speech. It is also economical which makes it fast-paced and much more punchy than the explanation which would be necessary with reported speech. You couldn't just write 'Stephen said his dog was a star', because the flat statement doesn't express his admiration and joy. The one brief exclamation expresses it all.

Direct speech gives a greater sense of immediacy than reported speech . . .

You are familiar with the adverb **immediately** meaning 'at once' or 'straightaway', e.g. *Come here immediately!*

In writing about media texts, make sure you can use and spell correctly the words **immediate** (adjective) and **immediacy** (noun).

A newspaper report tries to give you a sense of **immediacy**, the sense of being there and being involved. One of the ways a newspaper reporter can do this is to use **direct speech**. For example, in the report above:

'He's just wild about sea water! He'll always stand at the front of the deck where he'll catch the spray,' Stephen explained.

You could write:

In this direct speech the exclamation, the colloquial expression 'just wild about sea water', and the colloquial abbreviations such as 'he'll' are informal, lively, and immediate. They make the reader involved in the story. 'He'll always stand' gives a vivid image of the dog at the front of the deck enjoying the spray. It gives a sense of immediacy, as though it is happening <u>now</u> and the reader is in the boat with him.

Now, using different examples, write your own answer to question 1 above.

2 How does the headline 'Doggy paddles home' set the tone of the report?

Headlines are written to catch the attention of readers so that they buy and read the newspaper. Headlines often rely on humour and word-play (puns). Puns work through alternative meanings, or words which sound the same but have different meanings. Riddles and jokes are often puns:

—*Why don't cannibals eat clowns?*
— *Because they taste funny!*

This is a pun on 'funny' meaning 'peculiar', and 'funny' meaning 'humorous'.

Write down your own example of a pun.

To answer Question 2:

- ◆ explore the alternative meanings in this headline
- ◆ explain the tone of the headline (the tone is the mood, how it makes you feel – such as happy, depressed)
- ◆ say in what way the tone of the headline matches the tone of the newspaper report.

To practise thinking about headlines:

- ◆ Write your own alternative headline for this newspaper report.
- ◆ Write a sentence explaining your choice of words.
- ◆ Write the headline for a newspaper report covering a similar story, but this time, after the dog had swum ashore he died from exhaustion.
- ◆ Write a sentence explaining your choice of words.

Now write your answer to question 2 in full.

READING RESPONSE TO UNSEEN NON-FICTION

Making contrasts and comparisons

Text 1

Over one hundred years ago, in 1890, a 13-year-old English girl living with her family in Istanbul recorded an unusual event in her journal:

Istanbul, 19 February 1890

Today we experienced a strange phenomenon indeed. After luncheon we were sitting on the terrace when Mamma, Frederick, and I heard a queer, clicking noise. It grew so intrusive that we endeavoured to find out what it was. Imagine our astonishment when we saw that the sea was covered with thousands of heads of large fish! The clicking noise was the fish opening and shutting their mouths as they gasped for air.

Frederick and I approached the water's edge carefully for fear of frightening them all away, but we were astonished further when we saw that the sea had turned to ice and the fish were trapped. Our Greek servants joined us and great excitement prevailed as we proceeded to ladle fish after fish out of the sea until their weight broke our nets. Then with great dispatch we tied saucepans to broomsticks and shepherded the dazed fish onto the landing steps from where I filled my pinafore again and again with the harvest until the garden became a glittering mass of slithering bodies.

Soon men, women, and children arrived with an assortment of sacks and baskets and as I write this evening, they are still taking away all they can carry to pickle and salt for the winter. Papa says that in the morning the temperature in the water will rise and the fish will be released. He once saw such a phenomenon when he was a child but never since.

Text 2

Anthony Bourdain wrote in 2000 about Bigfoot, one of the restaurant bosses he worked for in New York:

In Bigfootland you showed up for work *fifteen minutes* before your shift. Period. Two minutes late? You lose the shift and are sent home. If you're on the train and it looks like it's running late? You get off the train at the next stop, inform Bigfoot of your pending lateness, and then get back on the next train. It's okay to call Bigfoot and say, 'Bigfoot, I was up all night smoking crack, sticking up liquor stores, drinking blood and worshipping Satan . . . I'm going to be a little late.' That's acceptable – once in a very great while. But *after* showing up late, try saying (even if true), 'Uh . . . Bigfoot, I was on my way to work and the President's limo crashed right into me . . . and I had to pull him out of the car, give him mouth-to-mouth . . . and like I saved the leader of the free world, man!' You, my friend, are fired.

I fondly recall how once, after a long-time waitress arrived late back from vacation, claiming her flight arrived fifteen minutes after scheduled time, Bigfoot called the airport to check her story and then fired her for lying. Treating Bigfoot like an idiot was always a big mistake. He lived for that. In the man's three or so decades in the life, he'd seen and heard every scam, every bullshit story, every trick, deception, ploy and gag that ever existed or that a human mind could conceive – and was always happy to prove that to anyone foolish enough to try.

These two texts are obviously entirely different. Continue this list of differences with as many as you can find:

Text 1	Text 2
written in 1890 by a girl	written in 2000 by a man
English	American
from a journal	from an autobiography
formal, descriptive, measured	fast, colloquial, witty

Comparing the writers' language

1 Vocabulary and expressions

◆ Text 1 has three-syllable, formal, educated words such as *phenomenon, endeavoured*; formal old-fashioned, nineteenth-century words and expressions such as *with great dispatch, pinafore, prevailed*; old-fashioned names such as *Mamma, Frederick*

    Text 2 has American colloquialisms such as *man, sticking up, Period, like I*

2 Sentence construction and punctuation

◆ Text 1 has complex sentences; multiple dependent clauses; accurate connectives reducing the need for commas; one effective exclamation mark

◆ Text 2 has racy, fast-paced structure in lists; full exploitation of direct speech; continuation dots; exclamations; dashes; brackets; italics; questions; short and long sentences used for specific effect

3 Use of qualifiers

◆ Text 1 has some conventionally placed, descriptive adjectives (such as *clicking; glittering*) and adverbs (*carefully*)

    Text 2 has few qualifiers but a succession of vigorous nouns and verbs

4 Tone

◆ Text 1 has controlled excitement; it is measured

◆ Text 2 has huge energy and pace, and wit through exaggeration.

Work through the four topics above and find your own examples. Next, make a comment on the **effect** of the features you are illustrating. Follow this simple plan:

1   make your language point
2   quote to illustrate it
3   comment on its effect.

For example:

> The formal, educated, polysyllabic words in Text 1 (**language point**) such as 'phenomenon' and 'endeavoured' (**illustration**) reflect the century and the high level of education of the girl writer, which would have included Latin (**its effect**). She wrote 'with great dispatch' when a girl now would probably write 'we hurriedly' or 'we rushed to' because the expression 'with great dispatch' (**illustration**) is now archaic (**language point**). These words are typical of nineteenth-century writing and give the feel of formality and control (**its effect**).

1   Now compare the writers' language further by commenting on the effect of the following words and phrases:

◆ Text 1: *great excitement prevailed; for fear of frightening them all away; shepherded*

◆ Text 2: *Bigfootland; your pending lateness; smoking crack; my friend*

2   How does the sentence structure in Text 1 and the sentence structure in Text 2 contribute to the distinctive tone of each text?

3   Select a language feature from each text and explain how it tells you something about the text's genre (nineteenth-century journal and twenty-first century American autobiography).

4   Why does the girl in Text 1 use an exclamation mark, and why does the writer of Text 2 use italics?

READING RESPONSE TO UNSEEN NON-FICTION

Reading the question and responding to key words

Read the following extract. In it Felicity Kendal, the actress, remembers when her mother had promised to give her a kitten for Christmas. But on Christmas Eve, the young Felicity realized that her mother had forgotten her promise.

Christmas Tom

Broken promises are part of growing up, but this was my first lesson and came, of all people, from my mother, who *always* kept her word. I went to bed in tears, and even the thought of other toys from the bazaar and a wonderful Christmas dinner in the big dining room, with turkey and Christmas pudding, did nothing to cheer up my little heart, aching for a tiny kitten to love and to play with.

The next morning I was woken by a hissing, spluttering basket, wobbling and shaking at the bottom of my bed. My heart pounded. I *loved* my mother – she had not forgotten after all! I scrambled to untie the basket and, as I did so, a large cream and black monster leapt out, spitting at me. It pounced on my head, fixing its sharp claws into my scalp, biting and scratching. My mouth was full of fur. It all happened so quickly that I had no time to defend myself. I felt no pain, just surprise. The beast was dragged off and my mother was called. She rushed in to see blood pouring down my face and my new pet crouching under the bed with its ears back, its tail swishing and its great blue Siamese eyes staring out from the darkness.

This was my 'kitten', this huge, nine-year-old, battle-scarred Siamese tomcat! There was a lot of washing of wounds with Dettol, but while my mother was sorry, she also seemed strangely determined to keep the creature, explaining that he was 'only frightened and would grow to love me'. But our first meeting set the tone for our relationship. The cat never loved me, in fact he hated me for the next five years of his life – and I hated him.

One of the most important examination skills is **reading the question** and **responding to key words**.

Read the first question on *Christmas Tom*:

1 How was the little girl feeling before she woke the next morning?

Write out the question and underline what you think are the key words. This means the words that are telling you how to answer the question.

How was the little girl _feeling_ _before she woke the next morning?_

First of all, the examiner wants to know about the girl's *feelings*. But the examiner wants to know about the girl's feelings only *before* the morning.

The second paragraph begins 'The next morning . . .' This means that if you include any of the girl's feelings in the text after this, your points will be irrelevant and earn no marks.

This makes your answer much easier, because it comes from the first paragraph only.

The writer doesn't, of course, say 'The girl was feeling sad . . .' You have to **select** what the writer does tell you and from this **interpret** how she was feeling.

Select relevantly from the text:

- her mother had broken her promise
- she was in tears
- thoughts of toys and Christmas dinner the next day didn't cheer her up
- her heart ached for a kitten
- she wanted the kitten to love and play with.

Now how can you **interpret** the girl's feelings from these selections?

- she felt that her mother had let her down; she felt betrayed by her mother
- she felt so unhappy and disappointed that she cried
- she was so deeply upset that nothing cheered her up; she couldn't be comforted; she was inconsolable
- her heart ached for a kitten; her whole being was taken over by longing for a kitten
- perhaps she was a lonely child, because she wanted a kitten to play with; perhaps she wanted a kitten to love even more now that she felt betrayed and deserted by her mother, whom she had always trusted.

Now, write your answer in full.

2   What were the little girl's first impressions of her new 'kitten'?

Write out the question, underlining the key words:

What were the little girl's <u>first impressions</u> of her new 'kitten'?

The little girl's first impressions of her 'kitten' would be how he appeared to her the very first time she saw him, and how she felt about him then. Would the following be relevant?

- her feelings the night before
- her mother's bathing of her wounds and reassurance
- the fact that the cat and the little girl hated each other for the next five years?

No, because these are all either before or after her *first* introduction to him. Go through the relevant paragraph beginning 'The next morning . . .' and write down what the girl first noticed and how she felt:

- noise and movement
- a leaping monster
- surprise, but not pain.

In your own words, expand these points, using detail from the text, to answer Question 2.

You can now answer Question 3 on your own:

3   How did the little girl's feelings towards the cat on Christmas morning 'set the tone' for their long-term relationship?

WRITING: ARGUE, PERSUADE, ADVISE

Arguing with flair and engaging your audience

Read this conclusion to an article by Andrew Marr. He is arguing that Britain is the best place to live in the world.

> We're hugely diverse, and getting more so: London alone has something like 350 language groups among its nearly eight million people. Yes, there have been pimple-outbreaks of racist politics but in general we have managed to mix and meld far more successfully than most continental countries. And if we have less countryside than many nations, it's also more varied – no place that extends from the Scottish islands to Norfolk's eerie flatness is dull, except to the dull-at-heart. Then there's the culture, the free museums, the great radio, the festivals.
>
> Alright, perhaps I'm getting carried away. Britain's not perfect.
>
> Compared to many European civilisations, we are horrible to our older people and unenlightened about our children. It's a mucky old island, and grumpy self-destructiveness is our least attractive trait. But by historical and geographical comparisons, we have rare freedom, prosperity, relative safety, a culture of tolerance, and energy.
>
> So it rains. Maybe it doesn't rain in paradise. But so far as this little green planet goes, I wake up each day, roll up the blinds, take a deep breath of London's chemical soup . . . and truly believe that this is as good as it gets.

The writer has presented his argument in a persuasive and readable way. Candidates frequently write their arguments for the examination in clear and accurate English, but their answers are often dull and lifeless. Such answers will not be awarded the highest marks.

What makes this writer's presentation so successful?

✓ Evidence, examples, facts, and illustration are reasonable and not over-exaggerated. They strengthen the impact of the points made:
   We're hugely diverse . . . London alone has something like 350 language groups . . .

✓ There is varied vocabulary – the contrast between colloquial or basic vocabulary and sophisticated vocabulary is used for deliberate effect:
   eerie flatness; culture of tolerance; mix and meld
   contrast effectively with
   mucky; grumpy; horrible.

✓ Variation of sentence length is used for effect:
   So it rains. (3 words) *But so far as this little green planet goes . . . this is as good as it gets.* (37 words with multiple main clauses and dependent clause)

✓ There is variation in punctuation, rather than just commas and full stops. There is a colon, a dash and continuation dots.

✓ Starting sentences with connectives adds force to the argument and retains the reader's attention:
   And if we have less countryside. . . But by historical and geographical comparisons. . .

✓ There is direct engagement with readers:
   Yes, . . .; Alright, perhaps . . . ; So it rains
   Words and phrases like these introduce ideas that tackle possible objections to the argument.

✓ Vigorous, lively, or hyphenated abstract nouns give 'muscle' to the writing:
  pimple-outbreaks; the dull-at-heart; trait; paradise; prosperity

✓ Its tone is persuasive, lively, and reasonable (rather than bullying or over-assertive), with the use of persuasive markers:
  Maybe *it doesn't rain in paradise;* **perhaps** *I'm getting carried away.*

✓ There is use of the first and third person:
  we have less countryside . . .; I'm getting carried away . . . ; It's a mucky old island

✓ Use of the first-person plural involves the reader:
  we have less countryside . . .; we have rare freedom

Now, you need to write a persuasive argument on whether it's great – or not – to live in the countryside, a city, a village, suburbia, a housing estate or a town. Choose one of these to write about.

Study the list of features above and experiment with writing effective sentences, using the text to help you. For example:

1: Direct engagement with the reader

Experiment with tackling your opponent's possible point of view as a way of strengthening your own. 'OK', 'Yes' and 'So' are useful initial words for engaging your readers in this way. Starting with connectives like 'And' and 'But', and asking direct questions, are also effective techniques.

> OK, so a city offers you fantastic pubs and shops to choose from. But it also gives you fast-food litter, clogged-up traffic, asthma, and crime. Wouldn't you rather have clean air and pollution-free sunsets?

> Yes, the countryside gives you beautiful views and new-born lambs. But have you ever tried to go shopping in Westville – or to get there by train? And have you heard those deafening tractors hour after hour?

2: Strengthening argument with personal pronouns

Experiment with using a range of pronouns for variety and for furthering the impact of your argument:

◆ use the impersonal third person for facts and evidence, e.g. *Crime figures are lower in villages; It seems that . . .*
◆ use the first-person singular, 'I', for strong opinion, e.g. *I'd swap shops and cinemas for roses round the door any day!*
◆ use the second-person plural, 'we', for including the audience in your beliefs and opinions, and thus getting them on your side, e.g. *How accurate is our image of housing estates? Have we all been watching too many television dramas about drug dealers on violent housing estates?*

Now write your argument on your chosen topic. Limit yourself to 300 words, and make every phrase work hard!

WRITING: ARGUE, PERSUADE, ADVISE

Organizing a persuasive argument

Read this extract from an article by the Hollywood screenwriter Joe Eszterhas. He has spent his career creating characters on screen who look 'cool' smoking cigarettes. Now that he has been diagnosed with throat cancer, he has realized that Hollywood has been guilty of promoting the poison of tobacco.

I have spent some time in the past year and a half in cancer wards. I have seen people gasp for air as a suctioning device cleaned their tracheas. I have heard myself wheezing horribly, unable to catch my breath, as a nurse begged me to breathe. I have seen an 18-year-old with throat cancer who had never smoked a single cigarette in his life. (His mother was a chain-smoker.)

I don't think smoking is every person's right any more. I think smoking should be as illegal as heroin. I'm no longer such a bad boy. I go to church on Sunday. I'm desperate to see my four boys grow up. I want to do everything I can to undo the damage I have done with my own big-screen words and images.

So I say to my colleagues in Hollywood: what we are doing by showing larger-than-life movie stars smoking on screen is glamorising smoking. What we are doing by glamorising smoking is unconscionable. We are the advertising agency and sales force for an industry that kills nearly 10,000 people daily.

A cigarette in the hands of a Hollywood star on screen is a gun aimed at a 12- or 14-year-old. (I was 12 when I started to smoke, a geeky immigrant kid who wanted so very much to be cool.) The gun will go off when the kid is an adult.

Read the text sentence by sentence. Think about the meaning of each sentence as you read.

Now work through these questions, writing down your answers:

1 In the first paragraph, the writer does not state whether or not he approves of smoking. How does he convey his opinion? In your answer, use these words: *evidence; example; shocking; statement; factual*

2 Explain the writer's opinions expressed in the second paragraph. Which words tell you that he is expressing an opinion and not merely stating a fact?

3 Explain the writer's wishes expressed in the second paragraph. How can you tell that his beliefs and behaviour have changed over the years?

4 In the third paragraph, what does 'glamorising smoking' mean?

5 In the third paragraph, what does the writer now believe is *unconscionable*? (You will probably need a dictionary to help you with the word *unconscionable*. Thinking of the word *conscience* will help you to understand its meaning.)

6 Write down a fact from the third paragraph which the writer uses to shock the reader.

7 Explain the metaphor involving the gun in the final paragraph. The metaphor is *sustained*, which means it is continued in more than one sentence. Refer to both the first and third sentences of this paragraph in your answer.

8 How effective do you think this metaphor is in making the writer's argument more powerful? Give detailed reasons.

Now, write your own argument piece. Instead of writing about smoking, you are to write three paragraphs about alcohol. You are going to argue that alcohol is a dangerous drug.

Use the following plan, and the example of the text above, to help you. Develop the points with your own detail. You might like to use words and phrases you have learned from the text in your own writing.

Paragraph 1:

Describe briefly a situation where someone is suffering from an alcohol-related illness. Select brief details which will shock your readers. Make it a personal experience, using the first person – 'I':

I have recently spent time in a hospital ward along with other patients whose livers have been damaged by alcohol abuse. In the next bed to me was young Tom, who had been living in the streets since his parents had found it impossible to deal with his alcoholism. Tom was only 25 years old, but looked like a haggard old man. He died the day before I came out.

Paragraph 2:

Express your opinion, provide persuasive evidence, and use persuasive language. Start with a link to the description in your first paragraph:

This was a shattering experience for me. I saw alcohol for what it really is.

Express your opinion clearly. These phrases will help you:

I believe; I think; in my judgement; I have come to believe; in my opinion

To persuade your readers, express your opinion emphatically. This means writing with strength and feeling. These words and phrases will help you:

passionately; absolutely; without a shadow of a doubt; doubtless

Give reasons and evidence for your opinion. Use some statistics to strengthen your argument, such as the number of people killed each year in the UK in drink-driving road accidents. Use emotive language to persuade:

slaughter; senseless; cruel; innocent

Paragraph 3:

In this paragraph, criticize advertisers for promoting alcohol and encouraging young people to drink. Start with a question, or even two, about advertising which will engage and challenge your readers:

How many more children will grow up to think drinking is cool before the advertising of alcohol is banned? How many more innocent children will have to be slaughtered on our roads?

Explain briefly that advertising encouraged you, or the sick person in your first paragraph, to drink alcopops at a young age. Finally, conclude with a point which shows you have thought about the issues involved, e.g. a suggestion for tackling the problem, such as banning all advertising of alcohol, refusing to treat people for alcohol-related illnesses on the NHS, or giving more help to alcoholics.

READING RESPONSE TO POETRY

Interpreting metaphor

Read this complete poem by the Cuban poet Nicolas Guillen. Cuba is a crescent-shaped island, one of the many islands in the Caribbean.

The Caribbean

In the aquarium in the Great Zoo,
swims the Caribbean.

This seagoing
and enigmatic animal
has a white crystal crescent,
a blue back, a green tail,
a belly of dense coral,
grey fins of cyclone speed.
In the aquarium, this inscription:
'Beware: it bites.'

The strength of a metaphor lies in the link between its literal and non-literal meanings. The Spanish poet Lorca expressed this idea when he described a metaphor as 'the leap that unites two worlds'. In this poem, you have to make a leap between a sea creature in an aquarium and what the poet is saying about his native island.

Write down detailed answers to the following questions:
1   Metaphorically, what is 'the Great Zoo'?
2   How are Cuba's geographical features 'translated' into the description of the creature in the aquarium? (You do not need to know anything about Cuba to answer this question – although it would be interesting for you to look it up in an atlas.)
3   How does the adjective 'enigmatic' prepare you for the metaphorical meaning of the poem?
4   The 'message' of the poem is in the last line – what does it mean, both literally and metaphorically?
5   How do the two 'b' sounds contribute to the tone of this 'message'?

A student has written the following response to the question:
Explain the metaphor in the poem *The Caribbean*.

The reader expects the 'Great Zoo' to be a zoo where species from all over the globe are kept and, literally, this is true in the poem. But within the first ten words, it is clear that the poet is using a metaphor: there is no creature called a 'Caribbean' and the adjective 'enigmatic' reinforces its sense of mystery and makes the reader curious. On a literal level, the fantasy sea creature is the shape of a shining 'white crystal crescent' with a 'blue back', 'green tail', red belly 'of dense coral' and 'grey fins'. With its bright colours, it sounds exotic and rare.

Metaphorically, however, this is a description of the island with its white sandy coastline, its coral reefs and cyclone-swept outcrops. The poet is describing his island, Cuba, and its people. The description of the blue sea and white beaches makes it sound like a stereotypical paradise island, but the force of the metaphor lies in the inscription in the last line: 'Beware: it bites'. Literally, this is the sort of notice to be seen in a zoo warning viewers not to go too close to the bars of an animal's cage. Metaphorically, the poet is making a clear political statement. Don't be fooled by the beauty of this island, he says, we are a fierce independent people and will not be the subjects of any other country. Be warned. We will fight if attacked or if any country tries to rule us.

An examiner has commented on this student's work:

✓ the initial explanation of the literal meaning is clear and brief
✓ the focus of the answer is on the interpretation of the metaphorical meaning
✓ there is a full appreciation of the metaphorical meaning
✓ the interpretation of metaphor shows insight and full understanding
✓ explanations are supported by embedded quotations which are both brief and apt
✓ the key metaphorical line is identified and quoted
✓ appropriate details are selected to develop interpretation and explanation.

Now answer the next question on your own:

Analyse the poem's structure. How does it contribute to the effect of the poem and its message?

Before writing your answer, it will be helpful to make notes on the following features:

◆ the number of lines and the effect of the poem's brevity
◆ the number of syllables in each line — what is the effect of the pattern, or absence of pattern?
◆ the structure of the sentences — are they simple or complex, and what is the effect?
◆ the vocabulary — is it emotive, factual, exotic, ordinary? What is its effect?
◆ the use of quotation marks — who's speaking? Who is 'it'?
◆ the consonant sounds — are they soft, mellifluous, harsh, plosives, sibilants? What are their effects?
◆ the vowel sounds — are they long, short, diphthongs, a random mixture? What effect do they give?
◆ the gap between the second and third lines — why is it there?

READING RESPONSE TO POETRY

Making an analytical language point

In your examination question on poetry, there will be an 'easy bit' where you will be tested on your basic understanding of the poem. You might have to explain what is going on in the poem, or the poem's atmosphere.

Then there will be the 'difficult bit' — *analysing the poet's language.*

The question might, for example, ask:

How does the poet's language convey the atmosphere of the poem?

Whatever the question is, it will require you to *analyse the poet's language.* This means you must:

1 Make a point about the poet's language:

The poet uses vivid similes to describe the fruit.

2 Select an appropriate example, and quote it correctly in quotation marks:

For example, he describes the apples as 'golden like the autumn sun'.

3 Explain how it achieves its effect:

This conveys the rich yellow colour of the apples in 'golden'. It also gives a feeling of warmth, ripeness, and richness, in the associations of 'autumn'.

Read the following verse from a poem by Ian McDonald. He was born in Trinidad and lives in Guyana.

Yusman Ali, Charcoal Seller

He grew rice and golden apples years ago.
He made an ordinary living by the long mud shore,
Laughed and drank like any other man and planned his four sons' glory.
His young eyes watched the white herons rise like flags
And the sun brightening on the morning water in the fields.
His life fell and broke like a brown jug on a stone.
In middle age his four sons drowned in one boat up a pleasant river.
The wife's heart cracked and Yusman Ali was alone, alone, alone.
Madness howled in his head. His green fields died.

Read this verse several times slowly and carefully.

Write your answer to this first, 'easy' question:

1 Describe Yusman Ali's life before and after his sons drowned.

You need to understand the content of the poem and select the appropriate information to answer the question. Use detail from the poem, but don't copy out chunks.

Now for the *language analysis.*

2 What does the word 'glory' tell you about Yusman Ali's plans for his sons?

When you have a question like this, break it down into smaller questions.

◆ What do you associate with the word 'glory'?
◆ The poet could have used the word 'future'. What is the difference *in the effect* of the word 'future' compared with the word 'glory'?
◆ What does this tell you about Yusman Ali's plans for his sons?

Here is one student's full response:

> 'Planned his four sons' glory' means that Yusman Ali planned for his sons' future. No doubt he wanted them to have a job and enough money to live on when they grew up. But the word 'glory' suggests he wanted more than that. It is associated with wonderful, stupendous things such as achieving 'glory' by doing outstandingly great deeds. By using this word 'glory' to describe what Yusman Ali planned for his sons, the poet tells us that the father planned brilliant achievements for his sons. It shows his enormous pride and love, which made their tragic deaths even more terrible for him.

3 Explain the effectiveness of a simile used by the poet.

◆ Select your simile – spell 'simile' correctly and copy the words accurately inside quotation marks:
> The poet uses the simile 'like a brown jug on a stone'.

◆ Explain what it means clearly and simply:
> The poet is describing the collapse of Yusman Ali's life after the tragic drowning of his sons. His life was broken into pieces and destroyed just like a jug dropped on a stone breaks into pieces.

◆ Now comment on the *effectiveness* of the simile. This means saying something about how the words work. Why a brown jug? Are the words 'fancy' or 'plain'? Why is that appropriate? What does the simile add?

> The simile is effective because it adds a vivid visual image. The reader can see the jug smashing on the stone and understand just how completely Yusman Ali's life was shattered by the tragedy. The brown jug adds to the picture of Yusman Ali's life as an ordinary man. The jug is a homely, familiar object and the language is plain and ordinary like his life.

Use everything you've worked through above to help you answer the following questions by yourself. Don't be satisfied with just one vague comment on the language – you will get no marks for that. Break the questions down into little questions and build up your answer bit by bit.

4 Explain the effectiveness of the simile in the line: 'His young eyes watched the white herons rise like flags'.
5 Comment on the effectiveness of the repetition in: 'Yusman Ali was alone, alone, alone.'
6 Explain the effectiveness of: 'Madness howled in his head'.

WRITING: ANALYSE, REVIEW, COMMENT

Analysing and commenting on beliefs and opinions

The people of Zanzibar, a large island off the east coast of Africa, believe that it is traditionally a place full of beings that can transform themselves into animals, and ghosts and spirits of all kinds. Here, two men from Zanzibar recount their personal experiences.

Text 1

Maruzuku

'I was sitting in my pick-up truck with my conductor. It was early morning and we were waiting in our usual place under the mango tree for passengers for the two-hour trip to town. The only sound was the birds screeching in the tree. My conductor was dozing as we waited.

'Suddenly, in a strange orange flash, the sun came out exceedingly bright. My conductor woke with a jolt and we saw that the back of the pick-up had filled with passengers. I got the engine started and we set off on our journey. Usually, there's plenty of chatter and noise from the passengers and squawking from the hens which they bring with them for market, but that day it was unusually quiet. Uncannily quiet. Halfway to town as we bowled along the empty road, we felt a sudden chill despite the sun. We looked into the back of the pick-up to check on our passengers. There wasn't a soul there. Not a soul.

'After that we never did the early morning trip again. I think the experience was some kind of message, some kind of warning.'

Text 2

Iddi

'I own one of the little kiosks by the beach. We used to stay open late for the night-workers such as the nurses from the nearby hospital, the taxi drivers and the fishermen. There was a good living to be made that way.

'One evening last year a couple of young men came to my kiosk on a motorbike. It was a big black machine and made quite a noise. Despite the fact it was a dark night, they were wearing sunglasses. They ate their chicken, chips, and chickpeas in silence, paid and then went to wash their hands in the bucket we provide for washing. But they walked straight past it to the big pot of boiling oil and immersed their hands in that. They never uttered a sound, but jumped onto their bike, kicked it into roaring life and rode off. A group of kiosk owners gathered round me and we watched in amazement as the motorbike made straight for the seashore – and the sea. After a few moments the sound and the bike disappeared beneath the sea. That was it.

'Now we open only until sunset. We think it was an omen.'

Analyse the content of these two testimonies by answering the following questions as fully as you can. Think carefully before you write your answers:

1 How were the men affected by their experiences?
2 Analyse the similarities between the stories.
3 Are these men telling the truth? Define 'the truth' in this context.
4 Give your reasons for believing or not believing that the men are telling the truth.

5   What do you believe happened on the two occasions?
6   Give your reasons for believing or not believing that these events actually occurred.
7   Suppose you dismissed the stories of these men as nonsense. Would you then be justified in saying that the men were lying? Give full reasons for your judgement.
8   Analyse the meanings of the following words and phrases, giving examples and illustrations to clarify your analysis: *to tell untruths*; *to fib*; *to lie*; *to misinform*; *to cheat*; *to tell a white lie*; *to be economical with the truth*.

Consider this question:

Comment on the belief held by many people that ghosts and spirits definitely exist.

Your personal experiences, your own character and interests, as well as your religious and cultural background, will affect whether or not *you* believe in ghosts. As far as writing a response to this question is concerned, it doesn't matter whether belief in ghosts and spirits is an important part of your life, or whether it seems ridiculous to you, or even repugnant. What matters is *how* you comment on the belief.

To comment fully, plan your answer in paragraphs. Include the following:

◆   a brief introduction explaining and defining the question
◆   a succinctly expressed analysis which shows an appreciation of the complexity of the topic, e.g. the possible existence of good and evil spirits; the problem of interpreting human experiences
◆   well-chosen illustrations from first-hand or second-hand experience, the media, or written sources, expressed economically and succinctly
◆   an appreciation of the range of issues involved, e.g. diverse religious and cultural beliefs; the need felt by human beings for support, comfort, and belief
◆   a considered analysis of both sides of the question, i.e. reasons for *believing* and *not believing* in ghosts and spirits
◆   a questioning of the key word 'definitely', which can develop your argument and analysis
◆   a sophisticated and developed vocabulary, e.g. *spirits*; *spiritual*; *atheist*; *pantheist*; *paranormal*; *subconscious*; *figments of the imagination*; *cerebral*; *vulnerable*; *dismiss*; *fundamental*
◆   varied verb tenses and moods, e.g. the conditional, with qualifying connectives for suggestion: *on the other hand, it could be; perhaps it would have been*; and the present tense qualified with an adverb for emphasis: *it is undoubtedly; I believe absolutely*
◆   an effective conclusion in which you recognize the diversity of responses to the question and give your own personal opinion of the belief. You are not trying to argue or persuade, you are concluding your analysis and exploration clearly and briefly: *For myself, I cannot believe absolutely in the presence of ghosts and spirits, but I accept that there might be a spiritual world out there about which I know nothing.*

WRITING: ANALYSE, REVIEW, COMMENT

Commenting and analysing opinions, and writing in continuous prose

Read this newspaper report:

Equality watchdog helps female pupils fight skirts-only rules

Like the other girls at St Robert of Newminster School, Katie Hunter is banned from wearing trousers. What makes her unusual is that she is determined to do something about it.

Katie, 15, will probably have left by the time the school, in Washington, Tyne and Wear, makes any concession. So far she has been unsuccessful. But that has not stopped her complaining to the Equal Opportunities Commission and the Education Secretary.

'The battle has already taken a long time, and I probably won't benefit from it,' said Katie, who has led a two-year campaign to get the trouser ban overturned. 'But I want to carry on for other people. First of all it's discrimination against girls. I feel I'm at a disadvantage to boys. Girls end up feeling the cold more and have restricted movement in skirts. The feeling I have had from girls at my school is that this is outdated and it's gone on long enough.'

Her mother Catherine cannot understand why the Roman Catholic school insists on skirts.

'Katie has worn trousers in every walk of life since she was a baby,' she said. 'It's a promise to her that I have made that we will see this one through. I just want her to have the choice, that's all. It's ridiculous in this day and age that we should have to ask for the right to do something that's accepted everywhere else. The answer we get is that trousers "don't look nice". But as far as I'm concerned it boils down to discrimination.'

The school said that the matter was under discussion.

---

1   Analyse and comment on Katie's point of view.

To **analyse** Katie's point of view, first write a list of the points she makes in her direct speech quoted in the report:

- she won't benefit from the lifting of the trouser ban; she wants to benefit girls who will come after her
- the battle has gone on a long time
- the trouser ban discriminates against girls
- girls feel cold and have restricted movement when wearing skirts
- the rule that girls should wear skirts is out of date and should end.

In the examination, making a bulleted list like the one above can help you organize your thoughts and your answer. Your final written work, however, must be in **continuous prose**. This means you must write in complete sentences and paragraphs. Don't use lists and bullet points.

You are explaining Katie's *point of view*, so use phrases such as *she thinks that*; *she believes that*; *in her point of view*; *she feels that* to introduce your points. The analysis has been started for you:

> Katie knows that she herself won't benefit from the lifting of the trouser ban, but she believes girls who come after her should benefit. She feels that the battle has been going on a long time . . .

Next, to **comment** on Katie's views, you do not need to select and explain the material in the text as you did for the analysis. You will use **your own** opinions and views. There are no right or wrong answers, but an examiner will want to read sensible and appropriate comments.

- Make developed, detailed comments, giving reasons and examples.
- Use phrases such as *I think*; *I believe*; *in my opinion*; *in my judgement*; *I feel* to introduce your comments.

For example:

> In my view, Katie's opinions are justified. I think that forcing girls to wear skirts when teachers and other schoolgirls are free to wear trousers is unreasonable and old-fashioned. I agree with her that the ban discriminates against girls. It's not fair that boys should be warm while girls are cold.

When you have written your own comments on Katie's views, you can answer the following question on your own. Use everything you have done for Question 1 as a guide:

2   Analyse and comment on the views of Katie's mother.

In the next question, you are going to **challenge** the headteacher of Katie's school by asking him to **comment** on points that you raise. **Comment** here means asking him what his opinion or view is:

3   Write down five challenging questions to ask Katie's headteacher.

- First, write a statement which sets out the opinion/fact/view you want to question him about.
- Then write the question, which asks for the headteacher's comments or view. Use nouns such as: *opinion*; *view*; *comment*; *judgement*; *discrimination* and adjectives such as: *incomprehensible*; *controversial*; *prejudiced*; *absurd*; *inappropriate*. Check your spellings of these words! Use a dictionary if you are unsure of their meanings.

Here are two examples:

> 1   It has been reported that you believe trousers 'don't look nice' on girls. (statement) Why do you hold this view? (question)
>
> 2   Almost all schools allow girls the right to wear trousers. (statement) How do you justify denying the girls in your school that right? (question)

Write your own five statements and questions. Check your full stops and question marks.

Finally, here is a task for you to complete on your own:

4   Analyse the advantages and disadvantages of having a compulsory school uniform.

- Start by making two headings, *Advantages* and *Disadvantages*.
- Make a list of bulleted or numbered points under each heading.
- Use this list to write out your points in **paragraphs** and in **continuous prose**.
- Use connecting words and phrases such as: *on the other hand*; *the opposite view*; *however*; *but*; *conversely*.

These pages show examples of the types of pre-released texts you will receive before your examinations. Printed here are the texts you need for answering the sample examination papers in this book.

Spend as much time as you like studying them and preparing for the examination questions.

Don't look at the examination papers until you are ready to give the correct length of time to them.

Section A: Media texts

Text 1

Sherpas risk death for British trekkers

Dozens of exploited porters die every year as travel firms cut costs
By David Harrison, Environment Correspondent

They are regarded as the heirs of Sherpa Tenzing, but dozens of porters who carry British trekkers' equipment in the Himalayas are dying every year because travel companies are exploiting them, according to an investigation by a London-based charity.

The organisation, Tourism Concern, claims that porters in Nepal, Tanzania and Peru die from hypothermia and altitude sickness because travel firms from Britain and other Western countries are 'cutting corners on cost'.

The charity says that many tour companies fail to supply porters with protective clothes and medical care, and force them to carry loads up to 130lb and sleep in the open in sub-zero temperatures.

The exact number of deaths is unknown since not all are recorded. It has been claimed that some bodies are not discovered until the snow melts, and that thousands of other porters suffer from frostbite and snowblindness, with one hospital in Nepal treating 2,000 carriers a year.

Most of the porters are not sherpas used to carrying equipment at high altitudes, but poor farmers desperate to boost their incomes. The alleged abuses took place on trips in the Himalayas, Kilimanjaro, and on the Inca Trail to Machu Picchu in Peru, all popular destinations for British trekkers.

Sherpas are treated as little more than beasts of burden without proper clothes or medical care, according to a British charity.

Lara Marsh, the charity's campaigns officer, said: 'Porters are dying because there is no respect for their lives. They are seen as beasts of burden. The abuse is shocking and it would be easy and inexpensive to stop it.'

The allegations include one regarding a Nepalese porter who is said to have had parts of his feet amputated after he got frostbite while working for a group on Everest. Kulbahadur Rai was 13,000ft up the mountain at Pheriche when he fell ill with altitude sickness. Instead of being taken down the mountain quickly, he carried his load to the next camp at an even higher altitude before making his own way down at night in a snowstorm. Back at Pheriche he collapsed and fell into a coma for nine days, before waking up in hospital.

Doug Scott, who runs a trekking company in Carlisle and has been travelling to the Himalayas for 30 years, said that porters were put at risk by companies taking the lowest quotes from local agents and failing to check how the porters were treated.

'Some of the companies perhaps don't realise that they are only getting cheaper deals because the porters are being treated badly. Some know and just don't care,' he said. 'This problem desperately needs to be addressed. It's incredible that so few tour operators are taking this seriously.'

Mr Scott quoted the example of a British school party 'from the South Coast' on a trekking holiday in the Himalayas. He said that the porters worked from 6am to 9pm, climbing with 88lb bags on their backs with no protective clothing. For their 15-hour day they received the equivalent of £1.10 each.

One British travel company executive, who spoke on condition of anonymity, said: 'We had no idea of the abuse because we hand over responsibility for porters to local agents. We will be reviewing our policy in light of this report.'

A spokesman for Abercrombie and Kent, the upmarket London company that organises treks in Tanzania, blamed 'middle-market firms' trying to keep their prices low. The spokesman said that the extra cost did not make much difference to the price of the holiday.

John Tefler, a spokesman for Explore Worldwide, an Aldershot travel company which sends 3,000 people a year on holidays requiring mountain porters, in Kilimanjaro, Peru and Nepal, said: 'This abuse exploits the porters and damages the quality of the holiday. Being with porters and talking to them about their lives is part of the trekking experience.'

A spokesman for Kuoni Travel said: 'We use porters employed by our own agent, but the evidence suggests there are some companies picking them up off the streets.'

Tourism Concern has drawn up guidelines with tour operators. It wants firms to provide porters with insurance, improved pay, medical care, maximum carrying loads and proper clothing and footwear. The charity is calling on trekkers to report companies that fail to comply.

Text 2

Dea Birkett reckons it's time we owned up about where we go on holiday and why we really go there

Are you a tourist or a traveller?

One day, there will be no more tourists. There will be adventurers, 'fieldwork assistants', 'exploraholics', 'volunteers', and of course 'travellers'. But the term tourist will be extinct. There might still be those who quietly slip away to foreign lands for nothing other than pure pleasure, but it will be a secretive and frowned upon activity. No one will want to own up to being *one of those*. It might even be illegal.

Bali and Burma are only extreme cases in a trend to prohibit tourists from entering certain areas. New names are being added to the list of territories where we should fear to tread. Tourism

Concern lists China, Botswana, Belize, Zanzibar, East Africa, Peru and Thailand as having areas that have been adversely affected by tourism. Tourists only wreak havoc. Tourists only destroy the natural environment. Tourists only emasculate local cultures. Tourists bring with them nothing but their money. They must be stopped at any price.

Less than 40 years ago, tourism was encouraged as an unquestionable good. With the arrival of package holidays and charter flights, tourism could at last be enjoyed by the masses. The United Nations declared 1967 as the

International Year of the Tourist. A resolution was passed recognising tourism as 'a basic and most desirable human activity, deserving the praise and encouragement of all peoples and all governments'. By the 1980s, tourism was the largest and fastest-growing industry in the world. By the end of that decade, 20 million Britons a year went abroad on holiday.

It won't be easy to wipe out this massive, ever growing tribe. Today there are more than 700m 'tourist arrivals' each year. The World Tourism Organisation (WTO) forecasts that, by 2020, there will be 1.56 billion tourists travelling at any one time. The challenge to forcibly curtail more than a billion tourists from going where they want to go is immense. It is so immense as to be impossible. You cannot make so many economically empowered people stop doing something they want to do unless you argue that it is of such extreme damage to the welfare of the world that only the truly malicious, utterly selfish and totally irresponsible would ever even consider doing it. This is clearly absurd. Whatever benefits or otherwise accrue from tourism, it is not, despite what a tiny minority might say, evil. It can cause harm. It can be morally neutral. And it can, occasionally be a force for great good.

So the tourist is being attacked by more subtle methods: by being re-branded in the hope we won't recognise it as the unattractive entity it once was. The word 'tourist' is being removed from anything that was once called a holiday in the pamphlet that was once called a holiday brochure.

As the tourist is re-branded, so the holiday has to follow. Adventurers, fieldwork assistants, exploraholics, volunteers and travellers don't go on holidays. Un-tourists (as I will call them) go on things called 'cultural experiences', 'expeditions', 'projects', 'mini-ventures' and, most tellingly, 'missions'. A Coral Cay Conservation Expedition flyer says: 'The mission of any Coral Cay Conservation Volunteer is to help sustain livelihoods and alleviate poverty'.

The word mission is apposite. While this re-branding is supposed to present a progressive, modernistic approach to travel, in fact it is firmly rooted in the Victorian experience. Like Victorian travellers, the modern day un-tourist insists that the main motive behind their adventure is to assist others. Whereas the mass tourist and the area they visit are condemned as anti-ethical and at loggerheads, the ethos of the un-tourist and the needs of the area they wander into are presumed to be in tune with each other. Environmental charity Earthwatch, which organises holidays for 'volunteers', assures that they will provide 'life-changing opportunities for you and the environment … See the world and give it a future.'

The re-packaging of tourism as meaningful, self-sacrificing travel is liberating. It allows you to go to all sorts of places that would be ethically out of bounds to a regular tourist under the guise of mission. Indeed, un-tourism relies upon exclusivity; it is all about preventing other people travelling in order that you might legitimise your own travels. Mass tourists are, by definition, excluded from partaking of this new kind of un-tourism. Pretending you are not doing something that you actually are – i.e. going on holiday – is at the heart of the un-tourist endeavour. Every aspect of the experience has to be disguised. So gone are the glossy brochures. Instead, the expeditions, projects and adventures are advertised in publications more likely to resemble magazines with a concern in ecological or cultural issues. The price is usually well hidden, as if there is a reluctance to admit that this is, in essence, a commercial transaction. There is something unedifying in having to pay to do good.

Text 3

Wild Wild West

Western Australia boasts a stunning city and a third of a continent of awesome empty country. Mark Brown goes walkabout

A drive out of Tom Price and you're in the Karijini national park, stunningly rugged terrain in the heart of the Pilbara region, one of the oldest land formations on earth. The Aboriginal people have lived here for 30,000 years, arriving by sea, it is thought, from the islands of what is now Indonesia.

The park's tourist centre, interesting though it is, is still very much a large tent, but by next year a new $3m centre should be open. But you don't come here for man-made things, you come here for the gorges, the stunning views, the walk through nature.

Our guide for the day was Tim Baird of Design-a-Tour (www.dat.com.au) who led us down red gorge paths, past shimmering white gum trees, paper trees, fig trees even, into subterranean aquamarine pools and waterways where you can swim, hang out and marvel at the beauty without another soul in sight.

Karijini is not full of tourists – only 35,000–40,000 come here each year, and most Western Australians are ignorant of the intense, breathtaking beauty of the place.

From Tom Price, we drove west through land rich in wildlife: kangaroos, emus and bungarras – a very fast 4ft long lizard which would not be out of place on the Walking with Dinosaurs set. If you want real outback, this is it.

Isolated sheep stations are increasingly opening their doors to tourists. We stayed at Giralia, 100km south of Exmouth. The place is massive, about 265,000 hectares with up to 25,000 sheep. Dinner, bed and breakfast costs between $50 and $90 a night. If you can't get in touch with your inner self here, then consider a clinic.

The vastness takes your breath away. It's a ferociously empty, beautiful land where the pioneers are still alive and working.

Another long drive and we're on the coast. Forget the clogged commercial beauty of the Great Barrier Reef on the east coast, the Ningaloo is, at 260km, the longest fringing reef in the world, protecting a lagoon teeming with the most incredible marine life. People here are rightly proud of the marine beauty and diversity – and anxious for it not to go the way of the reef on the other side of Australia.

The beaches could be from Bounty adverts – white sand, achingly gorgeous blue-green water, and, of course, the all-year sun. Along the reef, take your pick, there's so much room here. Turquoise Beach is popular with snorkellers and Osprey Bay is a fine place to just fall asleep.

We were based in Exmouth, a reinvented former naval base offering high-standard accommodation from as little as £20 a night. A backpacker can stay for about £6.

Neil McLeod, an archetypal outback man if ever there was one, operates a one-day safari for about £95 in his OKA – an ungainly Australian-built vehicle which seems to use tank engineering to create the coach that will go anywhere.

You will see a lot of kangaroos as you drive through western Australia, most of them, lamentably, dead by the road. But McLeod takes you to places you're not allowed, where there are large communities of kangaroos airily passing the time until spooked by something. They then get in a right fluster and hop crazily all over the place. You can, unfortunately, see why so many of them end up by the side of the road.

The highlight of the McLeod safari is Yardie Creek, 90km from Exmouth, which runs in from the ocean over a sand bank through intimidating vertical red rock. This is one of the few domains of the threatened black-footed rock wallaby which manages to survive in tight crevices and on impossibly small ledges. Seventy years ago, these timid, fascinating marsupials were abundant across Australia but proved easy prey, mostly killed off by foxes. No one's going to get them here.

Text 4

Wildlife pays price after drought sweeps Australia

By Nick Squires in Sydney

The worst drought in a generation is forcing farmers in parts of Australia to shoot kangaroos and emus as the animals compete with livestock for food and water.

Months without rain have turned much of eastern Australia into a brown and yellow chequerboard and forced wild animals to seek nourishment from lawns and gardens surrounding remote outback homesteads.

Feral pigs have also been on the rampage attacking newborn lambs and showing little fear of humans.

The animals, which weigh 110lb and resemble wild boars more than domestic pigs, have been considered a pest in Australia since they escaped from the farms or were released by early settlers.

Tom O'Keeffe, 71, who keeps 7,000 Merino sheep on a 30,000-acre property near the town of Walgett in New South Wales, said that he had shot a pig after he had seen it wander into a flock of sheep and grab the fattest lamb it could find.

'Pigs are ferocious,' he said. 'If they come across a sheep bogged down in the mud they will eat it alive.'

He said that the drought has left his farm looking desolate. 'There are swarms of emus all over the place and the kangaroos are dying of starvation.' Two-thirds of New South Wales has been declared an official drought area, and parts of Victoria, Queensland and South Australia are also suffering from abnormally dry conditions.

The lack of rain has been blamed on El Niño, the irregular movement of a large volume of warm water in the Pacific that disrupts usual weather patterns.

Some areas have not had significant rain for 18 months. Last week the state government of New South Wales announced emergency financial assistance but farmers criticised the move as too little, too late.

'I've been here 33 years and these are the worst conditions I can remember,' said Vikki Giblin, who with her husband, John, keeps 4,500 sheep and some cattle near Gulargambone in New South Wales. 'We have friends who are going

Dingoes starving in the drought are killed for attacking sheep.

out with rifles each evening and shooting kangaroos because they are eating all the grass.

'Another farmer found that emus were eating all the grain he was putting down for his sheep. He rounded up a big herd, shot them and burnt them.'

Although farmers are allowed to shoot common species of kangaroo if they have permits, emus are a protected species. Although once common, a recent survey by Birds Australia, the Australian equivalent of the RSPB, found that the birds' numbers have halved over the past 20 years.

Farmers say, however, that with their livelihoods at stake, they cannot afford to be sentimental about protecting wildlife. Many farmers face financial ruin and have had to sell some of their livestock, and others are feeding their sheep twigs and leaves.

'We had kangaroos eating the grass on our front lawn every night until we got a Jack Russell, which scared them off,' said Sue Davis, 38, who lives on a 69,000-acre farm on the New South Wales-Queensland border.

'None of us has much sympathy for the 'roos because they destroy all the crops and eat what little grass there is before the sheep can get at it.'

Nicola Beynon, from the animal welfare group Humane Society International, said: 'Drought places enormous stress on the ecosystem and brings wildlife into greater conflict with humans, but we don't think shooting is the answer. We need to find humane ways of dealing with the problem.'

Bertolt Brecht, a major figure in twentieth-century theatre, was a poet, playwright, and theatre director born in Germany. Hitler's rise to power forced him to leave Germany and he lived in exile, mostly in the USA, for fifteen years. He returned to Berlin in 1948.

The Label Emigrant

I always found the name false that they gave us: Emigrants.
That means those who leave their country. But we
Did not leave, of our own free will
Choosing another land. Nor did we enter
Into a land to stay there, if possible for ever.
Merely, we fled. We are driven out, banned.
Not a home, but an exile, shall the land be that took us in.
Restlessly we wait thus, as near as we can to the frontier
Awaiting the day of return, every smallest alteration
Observing beyond the boundary, zealously asking
Every arrival, forgetting nothing and giving up nothing
And also not forgetting anything which happened, forgiving nothing.
Ah, the silence of the Sound does not deceive us! We hear the shrieks
From the camps even here. Yes, we ourselves
Are almost like rumours of crimes, which escaped
Over the frontier. Every one of us
Who with torn shoes walks through the crowd
Bears witness to the shame which now defiles our land.
But none of us
Will stay here. The final word
Is yet unspoken.

Bertolt Brecht (1898–1956); translated by Stephen Spender

Shakuntala Hawoldar was born in Bombay, India. She emigrated to Mauritius, an island in the Indian Ocean, in 1967 and married a Mauritian. She has three children.

To My Little Girl

She was little,
She did not know the use of shoes;
I warned her of the brambles in the bush, in the briars,
She laughed trampling my words,
Briars, under naked feet;
She knows, I sighed
There are no shoes which she can wear for briars, brambles,
For she has seen me bleed,
Seen me bruised,
With my feet clothed and covered.

Shakuntala Hawoldar

MEDIA AND NON-FICTION
Paper 1 Tier F (Foundation)

Time allowed: 1 hour 40 minutes

Information

- The maximum mark for this paper is 60.
- Mark allocations are shown in brackets.
- You are reminded of the need for good English and clear presentation in your answers. All questions should be answered in continuous prose. Quality of language will be assessed in all answers.
- You will be assessed on the quality of your Reading in Section A.
- You will be assessed on the quality of your Writing in Section B.

To answer this paper you will need your pre-released texts on pages 32–37.

SECTION A: READING MEDIA AND NON-FICTION TEXTS

Answer *both* questions in this section.
You are advised to spend *60 minutes* on this section.

---

1 Media texts

Remind yourself of Media Texts 3 and 4 in your pre-released texts on pages 35–36. Write about these two media texts.

You must explain:
- the purpose of the writer of *Wild Wild West*, Text 3
- the effect of the direct speech and the picture in *Wildlife Pays Price*, Text 4
- the different ways in which the writers of Text 3 and Text 4 view wildlife.

(20 marks)

2 Non-fiction texts

Read *The Lobster Divers*, printed below.

Puerto Cabezas is a small coastal town in Central America. People are poor there. To earn money, divers risk their lives to dive for lobsters.

The Lobster Divers

The lobsters were collected at depths between 100 and 130 feet, and even taking it in turns to dive, the two men were working far beyond the accepted limits for safety and their health. Finally the team returned to deliver their catch, eat, and lie down on the open deck to rest while the air compressor shuddered and pounded through the night, recharging the air bottles for the next day of drudgery. If the weather was cold or rainy, the divers were allowed to lie on the wooden pallets in the hold. Next morning they were sent overboard again.

Acute unemployment in Puerto Cabezas drove the system. Lobster diving was the only legal way for the divers to earn cash. But the pay packets were meagre. The boat owners deducted for the air bottles, for the food, for the loan of the canoe, then paid a miserly rate for the lobsters. The owners also advanced money to the divers before a trip, and when the boat returned to port the diver often found he had not paid the debt, and was obliged to go to sea on the next lobster run. Much of the run was destined for 'Surf 'n' Turf' platters in restaurant chains in the United States where the clientele had no idea of the true cost. Occasionally a diver drowned. His canoeman lost sight of his bubble track, or he surfaced so exhausted that his colleague failed to reach him before he slipped back under the sea. Divers were slowly poisoned by the foul air they inhaled from the bottles, toxic with exhaust fumes from compressors. The divers were not supplied with depth meters to show how deep they were diving, or gauges to show how much air was left in the bottles. They had to guess. They received no formal instruction about the need for a controlled ascent to the surface, and at the rate of twelve bottles of air per day they were already operating beyond safe physical limits. Inevitably diver after diver suffered from nitrogen sickness, 'the bends'. Sometimes the onset was swift – a diver suddenly writhing in agony on the deck of the fishing boat as nitrogen bubbled in his blood. Much more often it was a cumulative effect with creeping joint failure leading to lower limb paralysis. There was no treatment and no cure. The nearest fully equipped compression chamber for treating 'the bends' was in Honduras – for the use of sports divers on sunshine holidays.

Tim Severn

Write about:
◆ **why the collecting of lobsters is dangerous for the divers**
◆ **how the writer uses language to involve the reader's feelings.**

(20 marks)

SECTION B: WRITING TO ARGUE, PERSUADE, ADVISE

Answer the question in this section.
You are advised to spend *40 minutes* on this section.

---

3   Elephants are still killed by poachers for their ivory tusks. Farmers often poison rabbits and foxes.

You are going to make a speech in your class debate. The topic is:

'Human beings *never* have the right to kill wild animals.'

Write out your speech, in full rather than in note form. Argue either *for* or *against* the statement.

(20 marks)

Remember:
◆ your purpose is to argue, persuade, advise
◆ to keep your audience in mind
◆ to write accurately and express yourself clearly.

POETRY AND WRITING TO ANALYSE, REVIEW, COMMENT
Paper 2 Tier F (Foundation)

Time allowed: 1 hour 30 minutes

Information
◆ The maximum mark for this paper is 40.
◆ Mark allocations are shown in brackets.
◆ You are reminded of the need for good English and clear presentation in your answers. All questions should be answered in continuous prose. Quality of language will be assessed in all answers.
◆ You will be assessed on the quality of your Reading in Section A.
◆ You will be assessed on the quality of your Writing in Section B.

To answer this paper you will need your pre-released poems on page 37.

SECTION A: READING POETRY FROM DIFFERENT CULTURES AND TRADITIONS

Answer the question in this section.
You are advised to spend *45 minutes* on this section.

---

1 Refer to the poem *To My Little Girl* from your pre-released poems on page 37.

Read the poem below, *The Day's Toil*.

This poem describes the hard daily work of a woman in Uganda, East Africa.

The Day's Toil

Wake up Woman!
The Cock is crowing;
It's three a.m.
Wake up – it's time to weed the fields
in the distant hills.
Sleep no more;
Arise from the burden of yesterday,
Forget the hours of toil
In that hot sun
That arose when you worked in the field
But set while you hurried to clear the weeds.
In the dark you return, as you left,
To those empty cooking pots.
Alas! the day is over
When the family enjoys the day's meal
But before you rest your feet
A voice calls: Woman get me hot water!
With that you know it's over
Until the cock crows

And the circle begins again:
Wake up Woman!
Wake up Woman!

Assumpta Acam-Oturu

Write about the two poems, *To My Little Girl* and *The Day's Toil*.

You must include:
- what the woman's daily work involves in *The Day's Toil*
- how the poet uses repetition and vocabulary for effect in *The Day's Toil*
- the ways in which the worries of the mother in *To My Little Girl* and the woman in *The Day's Toil* are similar and different.

(20 marks)

SECTION B: WRITING TO ANALYSE, REVIEW, COMMENT

Answer the question in this section.
You are advised to spend *45 minutes* on this section.

2 'If only I could win the Lottery . . .'

Many people believe that money brings happiness.

Write an article for your school magazine in which you analyse this point of view.

(20 marks)

Remember:
- your purpose is to analyse, review, comment
- to keep your audience in mind
- to write accurately and express yourself clearly.

MEDIA AND NON-FICTION
Paper 1 Tier H (Higher)

Time allowed: 1 hour 40 minutes

Information
◆ The maximum mark for this paper is 81.
◆ Mark allocations are shown in brackets.
◆ You are reminded of the need for good English and clear presentation in your answers. All questions should be answered in continuous prose. Quality of language will be assessed in all answers.
◆ You will be assessed on the quality of your Reading in Section A.
◆ You will be assessed on the quality of your Writing in Section B.

To answer this paper you will need your pre-released texts on pages 32–37.

SECTION A: READING MEDIA AND NON-FICTION TEXTS

Answer *both* questions in this section.
You are advised to spend *60 minutes* on this section.

---

1 Media texts

Remind yourself of Text 1 and Text 2 from your pre-released texts on pages 32–34.

Write your responses to the following bullet points:
◆ Explain what Dea Birkett means by an 'un-tourist' in Text 2.
◆ Comment on the effectiveness of the headlines, headings, and picture used in both texts.
◆ Explain briefly the sources of information which the writer uses in Text 1. Why does he use these particular sources?
◆ Analyse three examples of interesting language in Text 2.

(27 marks)

2 Non-fiction texts

Read *Edik in Malta*, which is printed below.

Edik is a young Russian. Life in Russia was hard and when he was given the opportunity to work in Malta, he thought it would be the beginning of a great new life for him.

Edik in Malta

Much later, Edik described his stay in Malta to me. Coming out of the airport building on a late autumn day, he was astonished by the heat. In Moscow it had snowed some weeks before; here it was still late summer. He took a gulp of salty Maltese air and thought to himself simply, I've made it.

The hotel had sent a car for him, driven by a laconic character who did not respond to Edik's attempts at conversation. So Edik sat quietly in his new cream mac with his briefcase tucked under his feet, and relaxed for the first time since he'd left Voronezh. Before they had left the urban sprawl that enclosed the airport, he was asleep.

When he woke more than an hour later, they were still winding their way through industrial estates, roundabouts and half-built tower blocks. 'Almost there,' said the driver finally, turning down a brand new road. They drove under a ranch-style gate, proclaiming 'Majestic Tourist Complex'. On the right was an area of waste ground pegged out with orange twine; up ahead a digger swivelled, depositing sand beside a concrete structure. The driver swerved around a pile of building materials and accelerated towards a white block with a sign: the Royal Hotel Malta. Here Edik had been employed as a night porter.

The next afternoon, a coachload of off-season holidaymakers arrived. Edik watched as they spilled rowdily into the foyer to be issued their room keys and a list of rules: 'It is forbidden to consume alcohol in the lifts and corridors. Guests are responsible for clearing up their own vomit. Any damage to room fittings is not covered by the package and must be paid for separately . . .' He went and changed into his hotel uniform – a cheap white shirt and black polyester trousers – and looked at himself in the mirror. After a moment's thought, he took out a small, sky-blue silk scarf and tied it around his neck, tucking it under his collar. Then he took up his post in reception.

For a month he watched drunken tourists retching into the ornamental fountain. They'd been promised sun and sea, but of course at that time of year there was not enough of the first and too much of the second, and the drinking took on a reckless edge. They thought Edik was hilarious. When he spoke his careful English to them, they hooted. The more generous gave him tips which made him blush. In his time off, he wandered through the souvenir shops and sunbathed when he could, although it gave him a rash.

When he returned, it was some time before we heard from him. His aunt returned from Kracow and there was no room for Edik in her flat. He came back to Voronezh and worked for a few weeks on an EU project, interpreting for two Germans, although he complained about them, saying, 'The Germans have a problem with taste.' Then, without saying goodbye, he disappeared to Moscow to stay with another cousin.

Charlotte Hobson

Why was Edik's stay in Malta disappointing for him? Explain how the writer uses detail to make her account vivid.

(27 marks)

SECTION B: WRITING TO ARGUE, PERSUADE, ADVISE

Answer the question in this section.
You are advised to spend *40 minutes* on this section.

3   There have been a number of tragedies on school trips and gap year
    expeditions recently. Parents and students feel strongly about
    whether or not such trips should be undertaken.

**Write an article for your school magazine in which you argue for or
against such trips. Give persuasive reasons and, finally, advise your
fellow students whether or not to go on one.**

(27 marks)

Remember:
◆ your purpose is to argue, persuade, advise
◆ to keep your audience in mind
◆ to write accurately and express yourself clearly.

POETRY AND WRITING TO ANALYSE, REVIEW, COMMENT
Paper 2 Tier H (Higher)

Time allowed: 1 hour 30 minutes

Information
- ◆ The maximum mark for this paper is 54.
- ◆ Mark allocations are shown in brackets.
- ◆ You are reminded of the need for good English and clear presentation in your answers. All questions should be answered in continuous prose. Quality of language will be assessed in all answers.
- ◆ You will be assessed on the quality of your Reading in Section A.
- ◆ You will be assessed on the quality of your Writing in Section B.

To answer this paper you will need your pre-released poems on page 37.

SECTION A: READING POETRY FROM DIFFERENT CULTURES AND TRADITIONS

Answer the question in this section.
You are advised to spend *45 minutes* on this section.

---

1   Remind yourself of the poem *The Label Emigrant* from your pre-released texts on page 37.

Read the poem *Exile,* below.

This poem explores the feelings of a girl when she comes from another country to live in England.

Exile

The old land swinging in her stomach
she must get to know this language
better – key words, sound patterns
wordgroups of fire and blood.

Try your classmates with
the English version of your name.
Maria. Try it.
Good afternoon. How are you?

I am fine. Your country –
you see it in a drop of water.
The last lesson they taught you there
was how to use a gun.

And now in stops and starts
you grow a second city in your head.
It is Christmas in this school.
Sarajevo is falling through

a forest of lit-up trees,
cards and decorations.
Mountains split with gunfire
swallow clouds, birds, sky.

Moniza Alvi

Write about the two poems by answering the following points:
◆ explain the girl's thoughts and feelings in *Exile*
◆ examine the effect of the rhythm and selected words in *Exile*
◆ compare the theme and tone of *Exile* and *The Label Emigrant*

(27 marks)

SECTION B: WRITING TO ANALYSE, REVIEW, COMMENT

Answer the question in this section.
You are advised to spend *45 minutes* on this section.

---

2   There have been letters in your local newspaper from parents and
    students who disagree over the usefulness of the Internet.

One parent wrote: 'It is a great pity the Internet was ever invented.'

**Write a letter to the Editor of your local newspaper in which you
analyse the advantages and disadvantages of the Internet and
comment on some of the views expressed in previous letters.**

(27 marks)

Remember:
◆ your purpose is to analyse, review, comment
◆ to keep your audience in mind
◆ to write accurately and express yourself clearly.

Contents

Here is a butterfly egg.

This egg was laid on a **fennel** plant by a Swallowtail butterfly. The egg is only as big as the top of a pin. It has a tough shell that stops the egg from drying out.

Inside the egg, a caterpillar is growing. When it hatches, it will feed on the **fennel** plant. This is a food of the Swallowtail caterpillar.

The egg hatches.

After two weeks, the caterpillar hatches. It is only 2mm long and as thin as a needle. It eats its way out of the egg with its sharp jaws. The caterpillar's first meal is some of the egg shell. This gives it the energy to find more food.

When the caterpillar has eaten enough of the egg shell, it moves away. Then it can start feeding on the plant. It is so small that its **predators** can hardly see it.

The caterpillar hides.

As the caterpillar grows bigger, its **predators** can see it and it has to hide. During the day, it feeds low down on the **fennel** plant so that it cannot be seen from the air.

At first, the Swallowtail caterpillar looks like a bird dropping, so birds ignore it. Ants are dangerous **predators**. They drag caterpillars back to their nest for their young to feed on.

The caterpillar changes colour.

The caterpillar is an eating machine. It feeds all the time. It uses its legs to cling to leaves and stems as it feeds on the **fennel** plant.

The caterpillar grows quickly. As it gets bigger it sheds its skin. After its third skin, the colour of the Swallowtail caterpillar changes to green. It is well **camouflaged** on the green plant.

The caterpillar is fully grown.

After four weeks, the caterpillar is fully grown. It is now about 50mm long and as thick as a pencil. It stops feeding and looks for a safe place where it can turn into a butterfly.

This caterpillar has found a plant stem. It spins a silk pad on the stem and grips it with its **tail hooks**. Then it spins a silk belt around its waist.

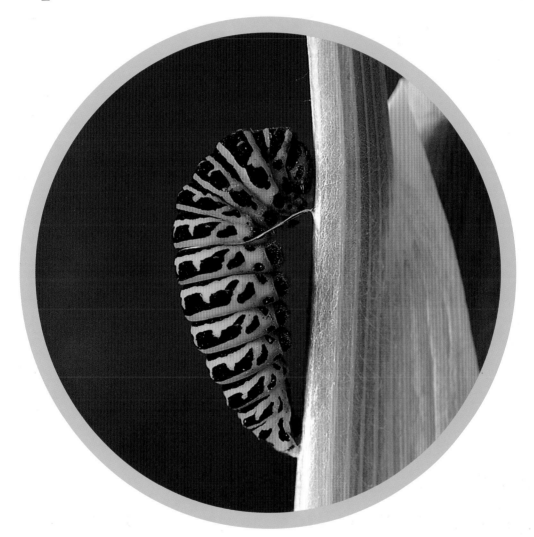

The silk is made by a special **gland** near the caterpillar's mouth and comes out through a hole called a **spinneret**.

The skin drops off.

After a couple of days the skin of the caterpillar splits and a case called a **chrysalis** (*say kriss-a-liss*) wriggles out. The old skin dries up and drops off.

Inside the **chrysalis**, the caterpillar is beginning to change into a butterfly. At first the **chrysalis** is soft, but after a day it becomes tough. The **chrysalis** looks like a leaf so **predators** leave it alone.

The chrysalis splits.

About three weeks later, the **chrysalis** becomes thinner and weaker. The wings of the butterfly growing inside can now be seen through the case. This makes the **chrysalis** look darker.

When the butterfly is ready, it pushes the top of the **chrysalis** with its head. The case splits open and the butterfly starts to crawl out.

The butterfly comes out.

The butterfly uses its sharp leg hooks to get a good grip on the plant stem and pull itself out of the **chrysalis**.

At first the butterfly's wings are wet and look like a small, damp cloth. The butterfly is tired and weak, so it rests on the **chrysalis**.

The butterfly's wings get bigger.

After the butterfly has rested for about 10 minutes, it starts to pump blood into its wings. This makes the wings expand (get bigger). The wings have soft **veins** in them, which carry the blood.

The **veins** must be filled with blood before they dry and harden. Otherwise the wings become misshapen and the butterfly won't be able to move them.

The butterfly's wings dry.

As soon as the wings have got bigger, the butterfly crawls to the top of the plant. It dries its wings as quickly as possible so it can fly. It has used up a lot of energy and needs to fly to find food.

The butterfly starts to open its wings. Their beautiful colours can now be seen. The wings' colourful pattern comes from tiny scales, which are arranged like the tiles on a roof.

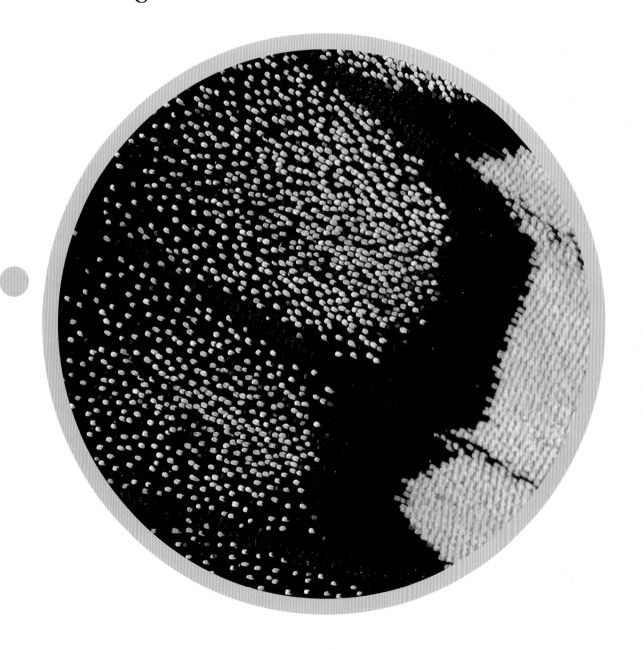

The butterfly feeds.

The butterfly can only fly when its
wing muscles are warm. To warm the
muscles, the butterfly moves its wings
up and down. Then it flies off
to look for food.

When the butterfly finds a flower, it feeds on the sweet **nectar** by sucking it up with its tongue. The tongue is a thin tube. When it is not being used, it is coiled up, just like a spring.

The male and female mate.

Two to three weeks after coming out from the **chrysalis**, on a warm, sunny day, the butterfly looks for a mate.

A female butterfly may be chased by several males before she decides which one to mate with. The female butterfly is fatter than the male because she has eggs inside her.

The female lays her eggs.

As soon as the butterflies have mated, the female butterfly flies off and looks for a **fennel** plant so she can lay her eggs. She will lay about 20 eggs.

One by one, she carefully glues each egg to the underside of the leaves of the plant. She spreads the eggs over several plants. This may take her a week. When all the eggs are laid, she dies.

Two weeks later, when her eggs hatch out, the new caterpillars will have the **fennel** plant to feed on.

Word bank

Camouflaged - When the colour and pattern of an animal's skin is similar to its surroundings, so it is hard to see. Camouflage helps an animal to hide.

Chrysalis - The case inside which a caterpillar changes into a butterfly or moth.

Fennel - A strong-smelling plant with yellow flowers. Fennel is a food of the Swallowtail caterpillar.

Gland - A part in an animal's body that makes chemicals for it to use. Caterpillars have a gland near their mouths which helps to make silk.

Nectar - A sweet, sugary liquid made by flowers. Nectar is a food for butterflies and other insects. Bees make honey from nectar.

Predators - Animals that hunt and eat other animals. A caterpillar's predators include birds, mice and some insects.

Spinneret - The hole near a caterpillar's mouth from which silk comes out.

Tail hooks - Small hooks at the back of the caterpillar that it uses to stay in place when becoming a butterfly.

Veins - The tiny tubes that carry blood around the body of an animal.

Life cycle

Two weeks after being laid, the egg hatches.

As soon as she has mated, the butterfly lays her eggs.

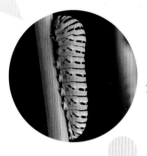

The caterpillar feeds all the time. It sheds its skin so it can keep growing.

Two weeks later, the butterfly mates.

After four weeks, the caterpillar gets ready to change into a butterfly.

The butterfly quickly dries its wings.

A few days later, the chrysalis wriggles out of the old skin.

After about three weeks, the butterfly crawls out of the chrysalis.

Index